NATIONAL GEOGRAPHIC

Ladders

LEND ME A PAW

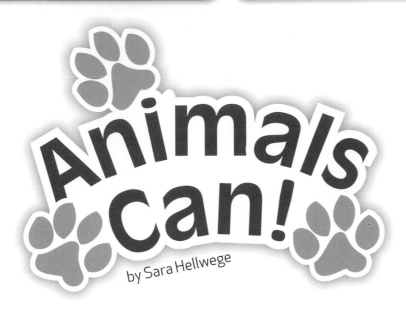

Animals Can!

by Sara Hellwege

It's a busy day. One worker guards a park to keep it safe.

Another worker leads a blind person down a sidewalk.

A third worker helps a patient in a hospital feel better.

Who are these workers? They are animals!

Therapy Animals

Friendly animals make many people smile. That's what animal **therapy** is all about. Therapy is something that heals or helps people feel better. Therapy animals are animals that help people feel better. Therapy dogs and their owners visit hospitals and nursing homes. Patients' moods improve around a happy dog. Many people who are stressed feel calm when they pet a dog's soft fur. Cats, rabbits, birds, and horses can be therapy animals, too.

A therapy animal needs to have the right **traits.** A trait is a quality that makes one thing different from another. Friendliness is a good trait for a therapy animal. Many dogs have this trait. That's why dogs are the most common therapy animal. More traits are listed below.

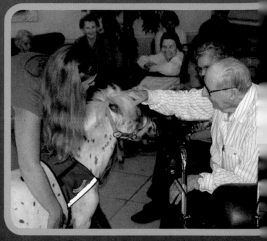

A therapy horse visits senior citizens.

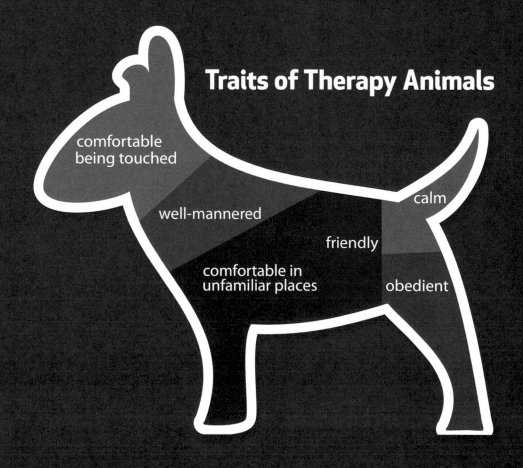

Traits of Therapy Animals

comfortable being touched

well-mannered

calm

friendly

comfortable in unfamiliar places

obedient

3

WORKING DOGS

GOLDEN RETRIEVER
Job: search and rescue dog
Traits: keen sense of smell

Working Dogs

Like traits, **instincts** are important for working animals. An instinct is a natural ability. Animals with certain instincts are good for certain jobs. Let's take a look at some instincts that help working dogs.

Herding dogs have an instinct to gather and move animals. They are taught **commands,** so they can do their job well.

Search and rescue dogs rely on their instinct to hunt. They use this instinct to find people who are missing. A strong sense of smell is a trait that helps them do their job. The dogs learn commands and are trained to follow a human scent. Then they're ready to go to work.

Guard dogs rely on their instinct to protect. They keep people, places, and animals safe. A loud, mean bark is a trait that helps them do their job. They are trained to use these instincts and traits at work.

BORDER COLLIE
Job: herd dog
Traits: nimble, loud bark

GERMAN SHEPHERD
Job: guard dog
Traits: strong, stern bark

Service Animals

Service animals help people. A service animal is a dog that is trained to help a person with a **disability.**

- Guide dogs help people who are blind get safely from place to place.

- Hearing dogs help people who are deaf by leading them to a sound.

- Assistance dogs help people with physical disabilities. They may pull a wheelchair or open a door.

LABRADOR RETRIEVER

Job: assistance dog
Traits: nimble, strong, instinctively helpful, intelligent

TERRIER

Job: hearing dog
Traits: alert, energetic, intelligent

Service animals are allowed in stores and other public places by U.S. law. The law gives service animals rights that other animals don't have. Service animals are working animals. If you see a service animal, you should follow these rules:

- Talk to the person, not to the dog.

- Don't pet the dog unless you get permission. Petting or talking to it can distract it from its job.

LABRADOR RETRIEVER

Job: guide dog
Traits: calm, not easily distracted, intelligent

Beasts of Burden

Some animals have heavy work to do. A pack animal carries loads and a draft animal pulls loads. Some animals do both.

In the past, people used animals to do work, but now animals are used only when vehicles can't be used. There are different work animals in different parts of the world. Let's take a look at a few.

Asian elephants used to clear land and carry logs in Southeast Asia. Cutting down trees is no longer allowed in many countries. Some elephants and their handlers now guard the forests.

Llamas have moved goods for hundreds of years in the Andes Mountains. They still work as pack animals today.

Camels carry heavy loads across the desert and can walk long distances.

Who can help people get hard work done? Animals can. So when you see a four-legged worker, say *thanks!*

An elephant moves a fallen tree in Thailand after the tsunami in 2004.

LLAMA
Job: pack animal
Traits: sure-footed in rocky, mountainous terrain
Location: Andes Mountains, South America

llama

ASIAN ELEPHANT
Job: pack animal and draft animal
Traits: strong, intelligent, flexible trunk
Location: India and Southeast Asia

BEASTS OF BURDEN

DROMEDARY CAMEL
Job: pack animal and draft animal
Traits: adapted for long-distance desert travel
Location: Northern Africa and the Middle East

camel

Check In What are some categories of working animals and what are the animals' traits and instincts?

THE NAVY MARINE MAMMAL PROGRAM

by Shannae Wilson

In the "Navy **Marine Mammal** Program," bottlenose dolphins and California sea lions take part in U.S. military operations. These marine mammals have special **traits.** These traits allow them to do certain underwater tasks better than people or equipment can.

Sea lions can hear and see very well under water.

Sea lions and dolphins are excellent divers. They can dive deeper and stay under water longer than people can.

The animals follow **commands** to do tasks. They protect ports, ships, and submarines from enemy swimmers. They also find dangerous objects under the water. Then the Navy can remove or avoid the objects.

The animals can be moved to locations all over the world. They have been used in past wars and conflicts.

Some people are in favor of the Navy Marine Mammal Program (pro) and others are against it (con).

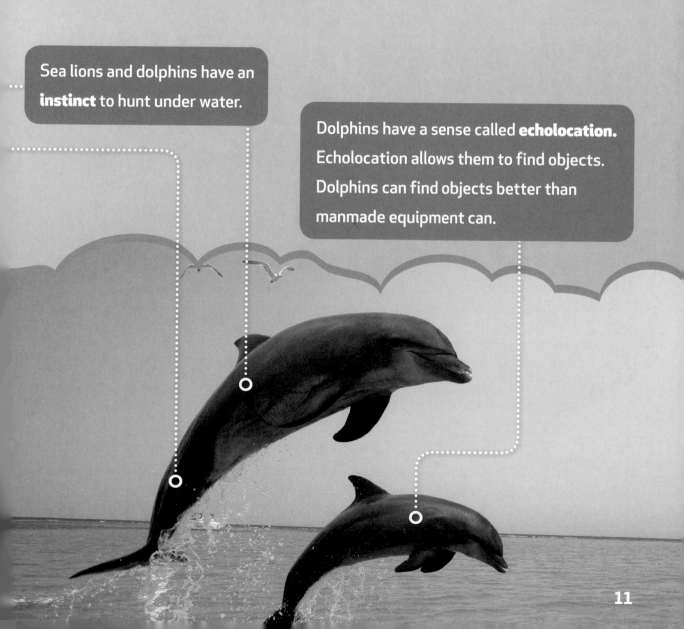

Sea lions and dolphins have an **instinct** to hunt under water.

Dolphins have a sense called **echolocation.** Echolocation allows them to find objects. Dolphins can find objects better than manmade equipment can.

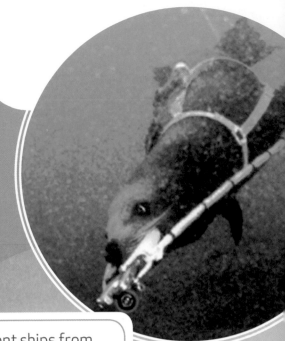

You should support the Navy Marine Mammal Program. It protects our troops and does not harm marine mammals.

1 First, dolphins and sea lions help prevent ships from being damaged or destroyed. They do this by finding dangerous objects.

2 Secondly, it is not likely that marine mammals will be harmed when looking for dangerous objects.

3 Finally, the marine mammals are well cared for. The animals live in clean enclosures. They eat a balanced diet. And they have regular physical exams by a veterinarian.

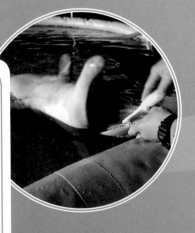

We should continue the Navy Marine Mammal Program. It helps protect our troops.

You should not support the Navy Marine Mammal Program. It puts marine mammals at risk.

① First, it's not possible to provide the proper habitat for dolphins in captivity. They are in pens most of the time. In nature, dolphins travel up to 50 miles a day in open water.

② Secondly, the capture of dolphins from the wild is harmful. Dolphins are taken away from their social groups. Also, some reports say that the capture of dolphins is hurtful.

We need to protect marine mammals. We should end the Navy Marine Mammal Program.

③ Finally, war is a human problem. Animals are innocent and should not be made to participate.

Check In Which opinion do you agree with? Think about and state your reasons.

One Smart Dog

by Beth Finke

Beth

Harper

Beth writes in her home office. Harper helps!

14

I'm blind. So I use my other senses to do things I enjoy, like writing books!

My computer has special technology for people who are blind. A robotic voice repeats the letters I type. It also reads what's on the screen. I can hear (and fix!) my mistakes.

I do most of my writing at home, but I travel to interview people and research stories. That's where Harper comes in. Harper is my Seeing Eye® dog. He was trained to guide me safely everywhere I need to go.

Seeing Eye School in Morristown, New Jersey

Golden Retriever mother and puppies

Harper was trained at the Seeing Eye School. Many schools teach guide dogs to help people who are blind. Only guide dogs trained at the Seeing Eye school can be called a "Seeing Eye dog." Dogs at the Seeing Eye school have **traits** that make them good guide dogs.

Harper went to live with a puppy raiser when he was seven weeks old. Harper's puppy raiser taught him "sit" and "down." He took Harper everywhere so he could see all sorts of people and places.

Puppy raisers must take dogs to crowded places, like baseball games.

After his first birthday, Harper went back to the school. Trainers spent four months teaching Harper to stop at stairs and at streets. Harper learned to judge traffic, and he was taught "left" and "right" and "forward."

Once Harper was ready, I flew to the Seeing Eye school to meet him. After practicing together for three weeks, I trusted Harper to keep me safe in traffic. So it was time to fly home.

Harper's ID card

OFFICIAL IDENTIFICATION

Ms. Beth Finke
and Seeing Eye* dog
HARPER
are graduates of The Seeing Eye.
This card is not transferable.
Expires: **12/31/2013**

James G. Kutsch Jr

James A. Kutsch, Jr.
President

Harper is always eager to eat.

Harper waits until he gets a command.

Then he eats. Yum!

I feed and take care of Harper. It helps build a bond between us. Every morning I feed Harper a cup of cup of dog food. Then we get ready to go outside. Harper and I use two pieces of equipment to get around. We use a leash and a harness with a sturdy handle for me to grab. I put Harper's leash and harness on him and command, "Harper, forward!" When we get to Harper's favorite tree, I unbuckle his harness. Then he knows it's okay to empty. (That's a nice word for *pee* and *poop*.)

Back home, I unbuckle Harper's harness and go to the kitchen sink. I lift his water bowl, and if it feels light, I know it's empty. I turn the water on and fill the bowl until it's heavy. I groom Harper every day, and when our workday is over we play tug-of-war and fetch with his favorite toys.

Beth uses a brush to groom Harper.

Harper loves to play.

19

Harper guides Beth across a street.

Good Dog!

Imagine you can't see. Here's how to travel down a street with a Seeing Eye dog.

- Lift the harness handle with your left hand.
- Face the direction you want to go.
- Say your dog's name and command, "Forward!"
- Your dog will pull you forward.
- When your dog stops, you stop, too.
- Slide your foot forward to figure out why the dog stopped. Did you feel a curb? Praise your dog. He saved you from falling.

Seeing Eye dogs fight their natural **instincts** to chase and sniff while they're working. Harper might forget to stop at the curb if he gets distracted.

Dogs are color blind, so Harper can't tell if the stoplight is red or green. It's my job to judge when it's safe to cross the street. When it sounds like the traffic is going the direction I want to go, I guess that the light is green. "Harper, forward!" Then Harper must decide whether it's safe to pull me across.

Harper stays put if he doesn't think it's safe. I can repeat the command and urge him forward. But Harper won't budge. Not until it's safe.

Let me tell you about **intelligent disobedience,** or refusing a dangerous command. Intelligent disobedience is the most difficult skill a Seeing Eye dog must learn. I'll leave you with a great example of intelligent disobedience.

Harper and I were walking on a city sidewalk. All of a sudden, he stopped.

I felt ahead with my foot. Nothing there. I waved my arm in front of me. Nothing there either.

"Harper, forward!" I urged. Harper did not move.

"Right, right!" I tried. No luck.

Just then I heard a truck door slam. Someone hurried toward us. "Watch out, ma'am!" The truck driver offered his arm. "They just called me to come fix this door!" He guided us into the street and back onto the sidewalk. "There's glass all over the place!"

The plate glass door had shattered. I couldn't have known this. But Harper did.

"That's one smart dog," our new friend told me. Thanks," I agreed. "I think so, too!"

Harper watches for obstacles ahead.

That's one smart dog!

Discuss Text Structure, Details, and Examples

1. Describe how "Animals Can!" is organized. How does the organization help you compare information about the animals?

2. How are the opinions organized in "The Navy Marine Mammal Program"?

3. What reasons and evidence are presented to support the two differing opinions in "The Navy Marine Mammal Program"?

4. Think of an animal that you know, such as a pet. What kind of job would it be suited for? Explain why. Refer to details and examples from "Animals Can!"

5. What do you still wonder about working animals? What more would you like to find out?